Go Green with Sesame Street

TRASH THAT TRASH, ELMO AND ABBY!

Mary Lindeen

Lerner Publications ◆ Minneapolis

Cooperating and sharing are an important part of *Sesame Street*—and of taking care of our planet. We all share Earth, so it's up to all of us to take care of it together. The *Go Green with Sesame Street*® books cover everything from appreciating Earth's beauty, to conserving its resources, to helping keep it clean, and more. And the familiar, furry friends from *Sesame Street* offer young readers some easy ways to help protect their planet.

Sincerely,

The Editors at Sesame Workshop

The text of this book is printed on paper that is made with 30 percent recycled postconsumer waste fibers.

Table of Contents

Our Beautiful Earth

Look around.
Earth is so beautiful!

There are so many pretty things to see! How can Elmo and Abby help keep Earth beautiful?

We can put trash where it belongs, Elmo!

Lots of Litter

Some places on Earth are clean. But some places have litter. Earth does not look beautiful with litter.

Litter is trash that is left in places where it doesn't belong. Cans, bottles, and food can all be litter.

All kinds of things can be litter!

Where Does Litter Come From?

Sometimes people drop trash as they walk.
Or they leave it where they were sitting.

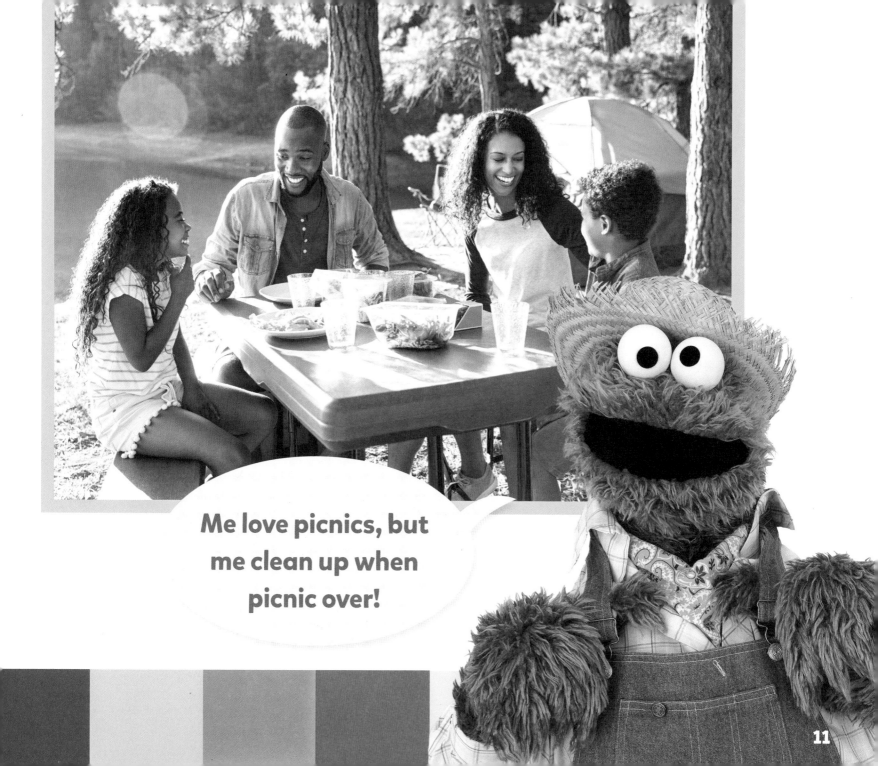

Me love picnics, but me clean up when picnic over!

Some people throw trash out of their cars. That is not where trash belongs.

Litter is bad for people and animals.
Animals might eat litter if it is in their space.

Let's work together to stop litter from hurting animals!

Cleaning Up Litter

You can help stop litter before it starts.

Elmo can stop litter. And you can too!

Always put your trash where it belongs.

Some trash, such as plastic bottles or paper, can be recycled. They can be made into something new. Put this trash in the recycling bin.

The recycling bin has a triangle made of arrows.

You help Earth when you pick up litter. Everyone can help.

You can pick up papers and wrappers. But leave litter with sharp edges for an adult.

Ask an adult if something seems unsafe to pick up. Wear gloves if you can.

Always wash your hands when you're done picking up litter.

Everyone can help pick up litter. We can work together to keep our world clean.

Picking up litter makes Earth cleaner, healthier, and more beautiful. A clean planet is a better home for everybody!

Earth Day Every Day

Earth Day is a special day each year when people celebrate Earth. It happens on April 22.

We love Earth Day!

Some people celebrate by picking up litter.
It's a great way to take care of Earth!

A Cool School Cleanup

You and your friends can clean up litter around your school.

1. Check with your teacher to make sure it's okay to have a cleanup day.

2. Put up some signs to let everyone know when you're going to clean up. Ask both kids and adults to help.

3. Remember to wear gloves and stay safe. Ask an adult for help with anything that you're not sure about.

4. Put all the litter in the trash can or recycling bin. Then wash your hands and enjoy your cool, cleaned-up school!

Glossary

healthier: more healthy

litter: trash that is left in places where it doesn't belong

recycled: made into something new

recycling: an item that can be made into something new

For Benjamin, who makes my world more wonderful every day

Index

Photo Acknowledgments

Additional image credits: grimgram/Getty Images, throughout (trash); vectortatu/Shutterstock.com, throughout (background); mauruson/Getty Images, p. 2; TinnaPong/Shutterstock.com, p. 5; AlinaMD/Getty Images, p. 6; Carlos Ciudad Photography/Getty Images, p. 7; Monty Rakusen/Getty Images, p. 8; FrankieMea/Getty Images, p. 9; PinkBadger/Getty Images, p. 10; monkeybusinessimages/Getty Images, p. 11; Chev Wilkinson/Getty Images, p. 12; ozgurcoskun/Getty Images, p. 13; Willyam Bradberry/Shutterstock.com, p. 14; Sasiistock/Getty Images, p. 17; FatCamera/Getty Images, p. 18; SolStock/Getty Images, p. 20; Ariel Skelley/Getty Images, p. 23; fstop123/Getty Images, pp. 24, 29, 30; Lane Oatey/Blue Jean Images/Getty Images, p. 26. Cover: style_TTT/Shutterstock.com (background), mauruson/Getty Images (trash).

Lerner Publications Company
An imprint of Lerner Publishing Group, Inc.
241 First Avenue North
Minneapolis, MN 55401 USA

For reading levels and more information, look up this title at www.lernerbooks.com.

Main body text set in Mikado.
Typeface provided by HVD.

Library of Congress Cataloging-in-Publication Data

Names: Lindeen, Mary, author.
Title: Trash that trash, Elmo and Abby! / Mary Lindeen.
Description: Minneapolis : Lerner Publications, [2020] | Series: Go green with Sesame Street | Includes bibliographical references and index.
Identifiers: LCCN 2019012419 (print) | LCCN 2019016932 (ebook) | ISBN 9781541583115 (eb pdf) | ISBN 9781541572584 (lib. bdg. : alk. paper)
Subjects: LCSH: Litter (Trash)—Juvenile literature. | Refuse and refuse disposal—Juvenile literature. | Sesame Street (Television program)—Juvenile literature.
Classification: LCC TD813 (ebook) | LCC TD813 .L56 2020 (print) | DDC 363.72/8—dc23

LC record available at https://lccn.loc.gov/2019012419

Manufactured in the United States of America
1-46525-47570-7/9/2019